The Dinner Party

A book by RL Lane

"A girlfriend will bring the ice cream when it's time to chat. A girlfriend will yell at you when you are wrong. Guys should have girlfriends." RL Lane

Introduction: "secret Life OV an antE". LOVE love love love love. Follow the love…

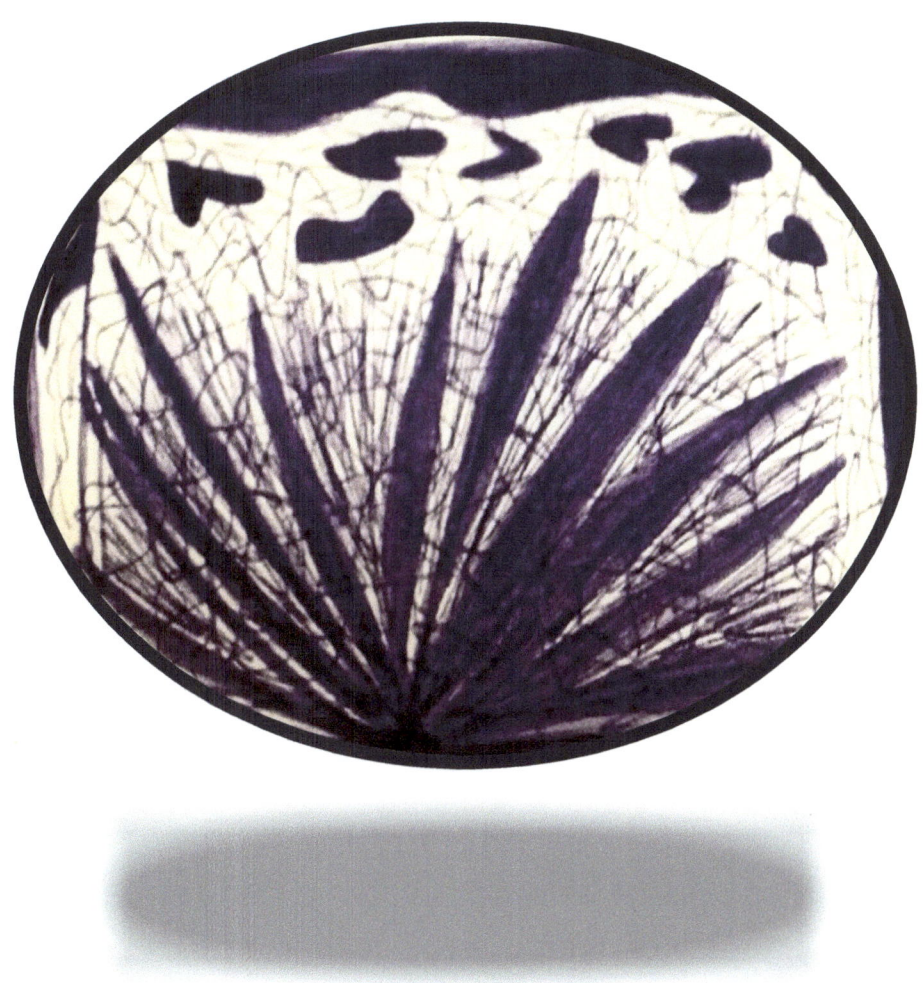

Grains of wood I see. A pencil to draw with so you can see…

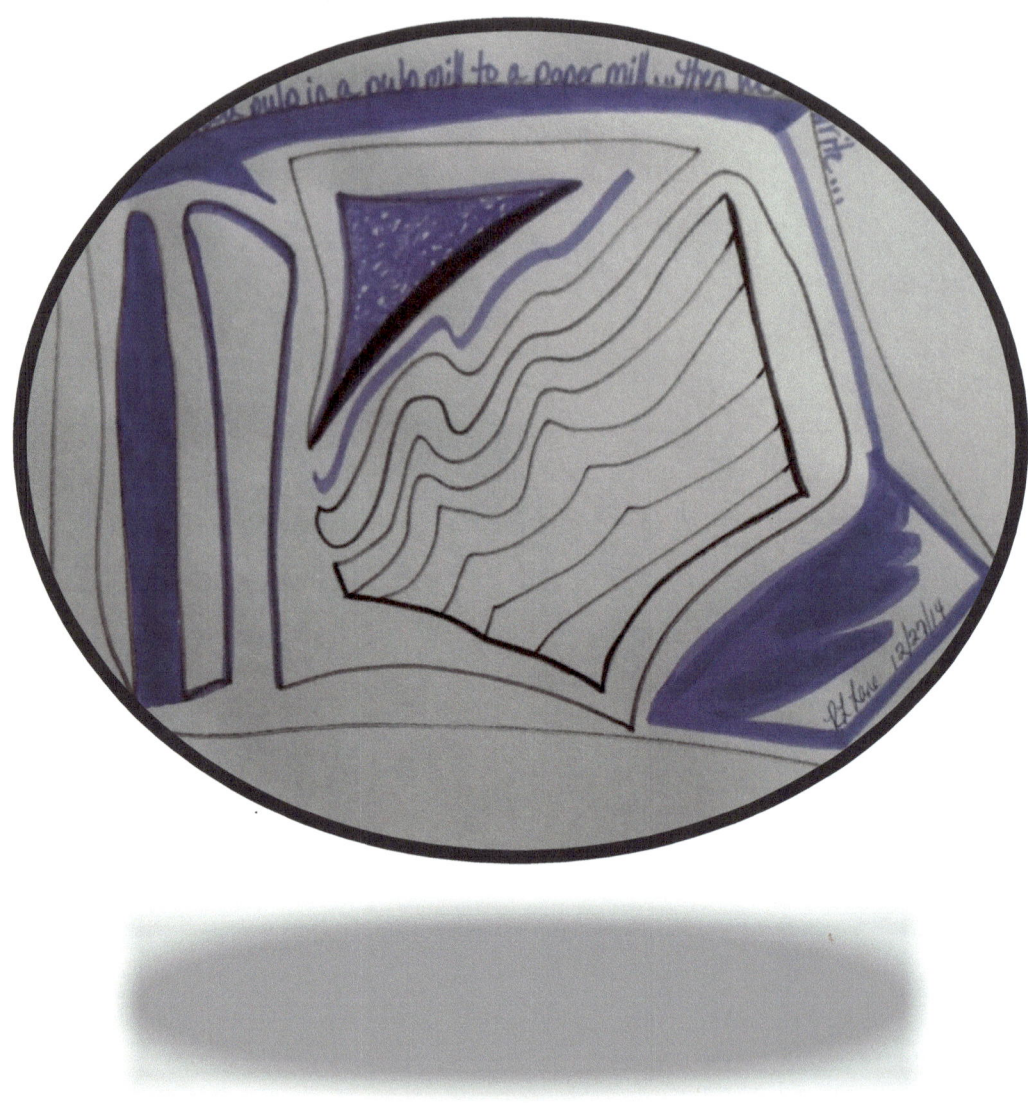

From wood to wood pulp in a pulp mill to a paper mill…then we write…

He was late with the delivery. The wagon wheels did not turn fast enough.
The saloon owner knew his customers would need their drink…

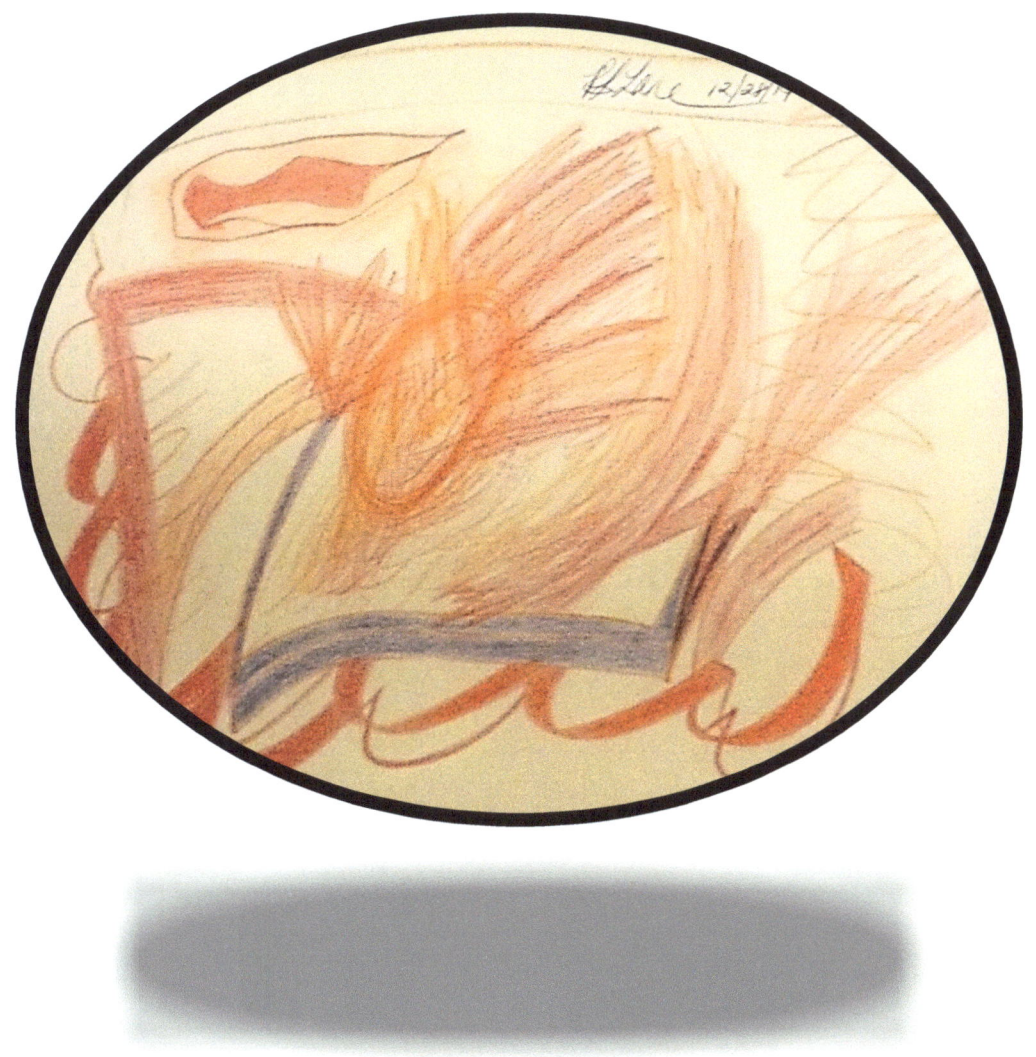

Why do those saloons have swinging doors? Is it so they can easily stumble out?

The birdman sits in his tree…he sings and sings his song. Sound the horn…follow the path up the tree…

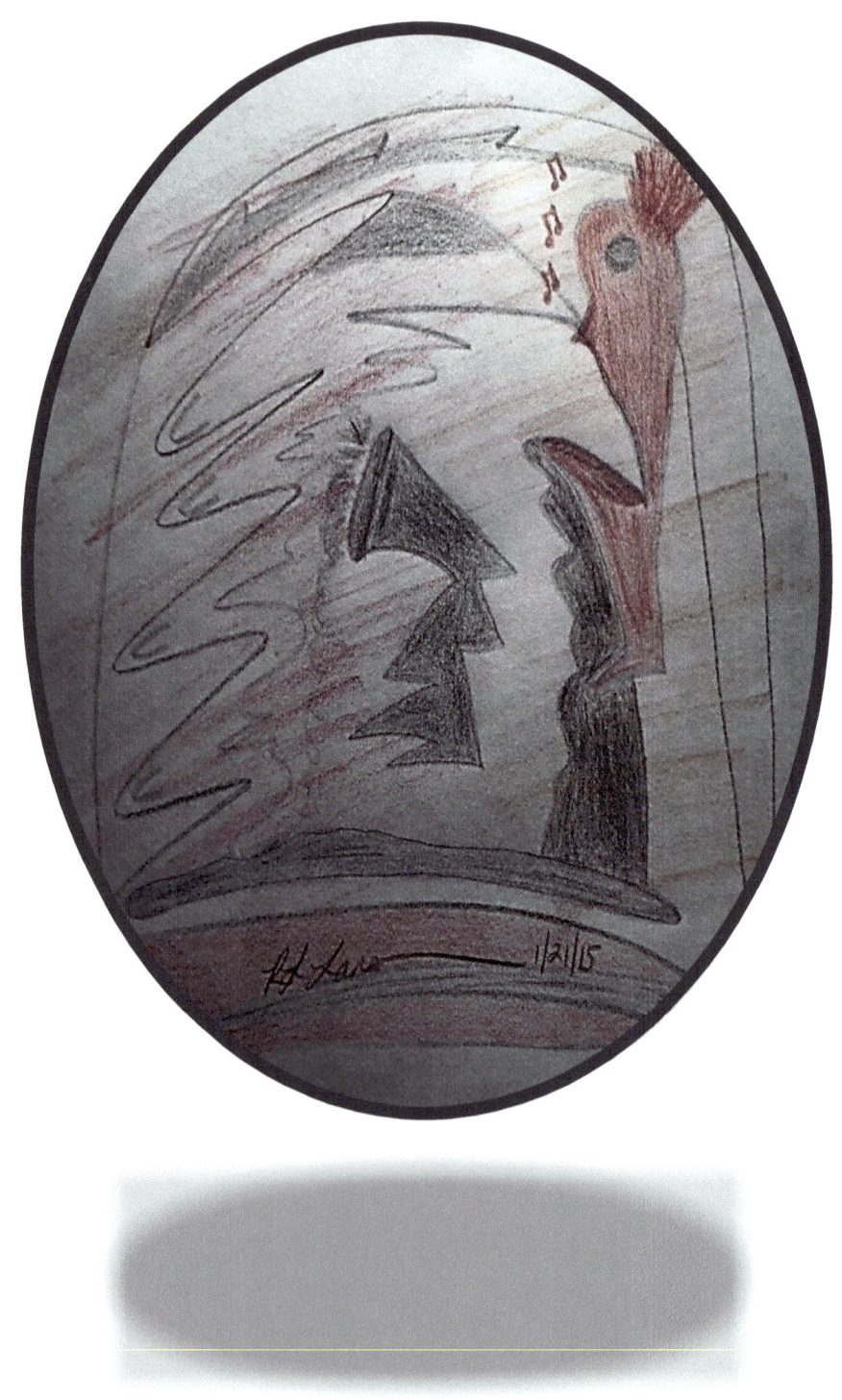

Poor Mrs. Greenthumb. She was working hard in her garden when she got her green thumb…

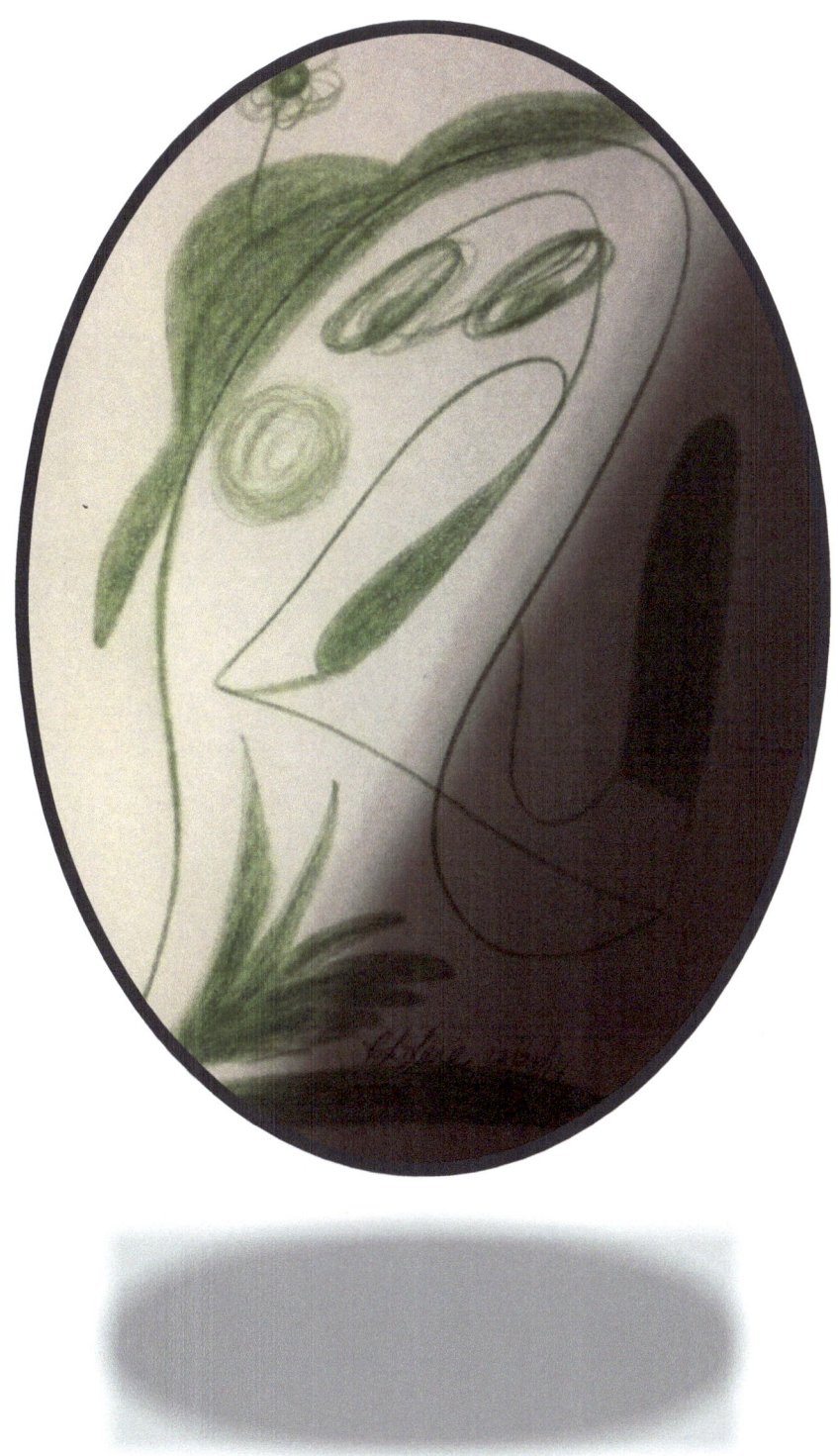

They showed me The Dinner Party. They knew I needed help. I needed to beli ve. They showed me the long table. So long that it curved around to the left into the room…

All the friends were there. The ones who become part of my book world. I was sitting at the end. I went back to get slices of meat. Oh. I will have teeth at the end my life. I will still be able to chew meat...

Then someone handed me a strawberry ice cream cone with mincemeat in it. I told them my Mom loved mincemeat. Oh. I will be finding connections for the rest of my life...

I was happy sitting there looking around at the friends who helped RL Lane. The ones who beli ved in her. There were so many friends. I really could not see the end of the table. As usual, I was there in person, but slightly off somewhere else…

Then he arrived before the party was over. People immediately went to talk to him. They wanted to hear what he had to say. I sat there and listened to his beautiful voice. An old voice full of wisdom. I loved to hear its sound…

They showed me my soul mate so I know he does find me…

They showed me book world so I will know it does become real…

I loved this drawing, but it took me months to see the real picture…

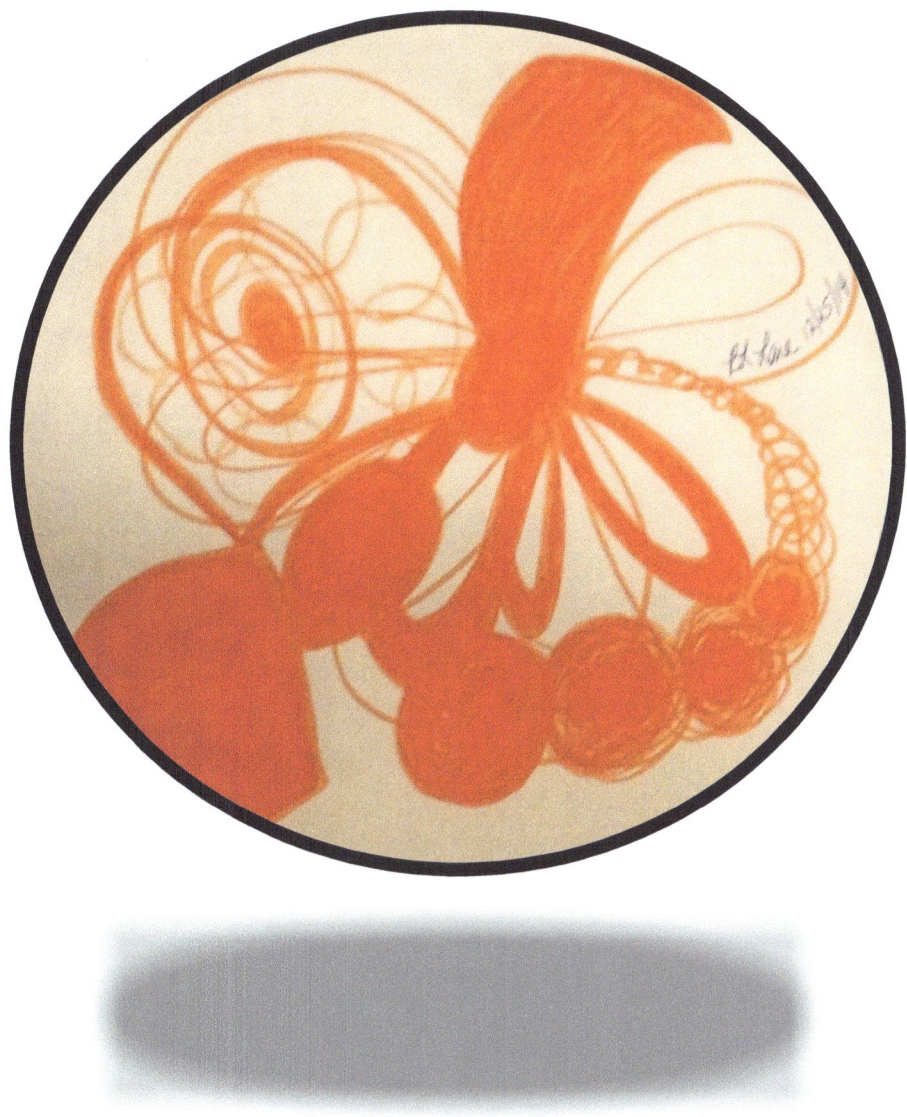

I called it "lobster bow".

It really goes like this…

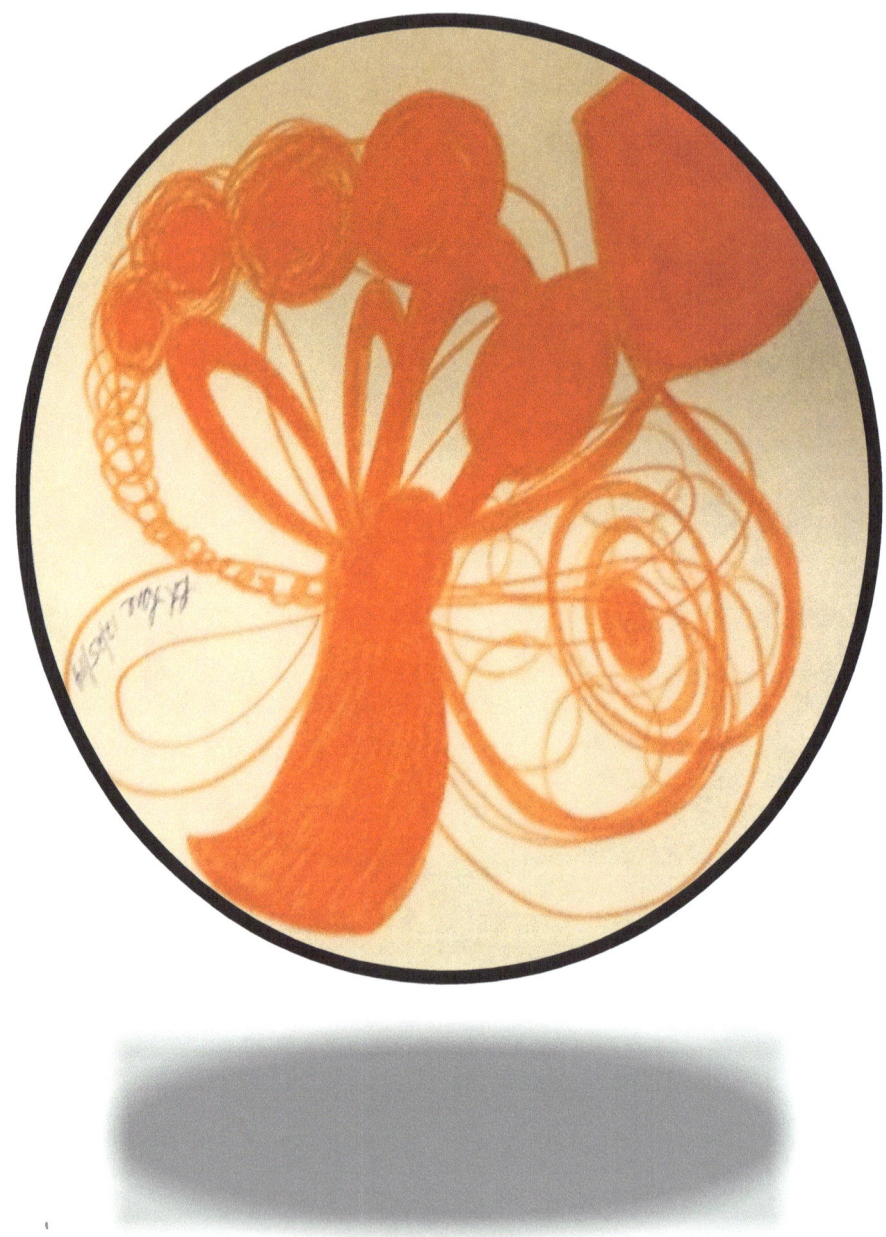

Her angel Mom with butterfly wings, making a nest or web, most likely both, for her 4 babies…

Come along for the ride… I promise my brain can do it…

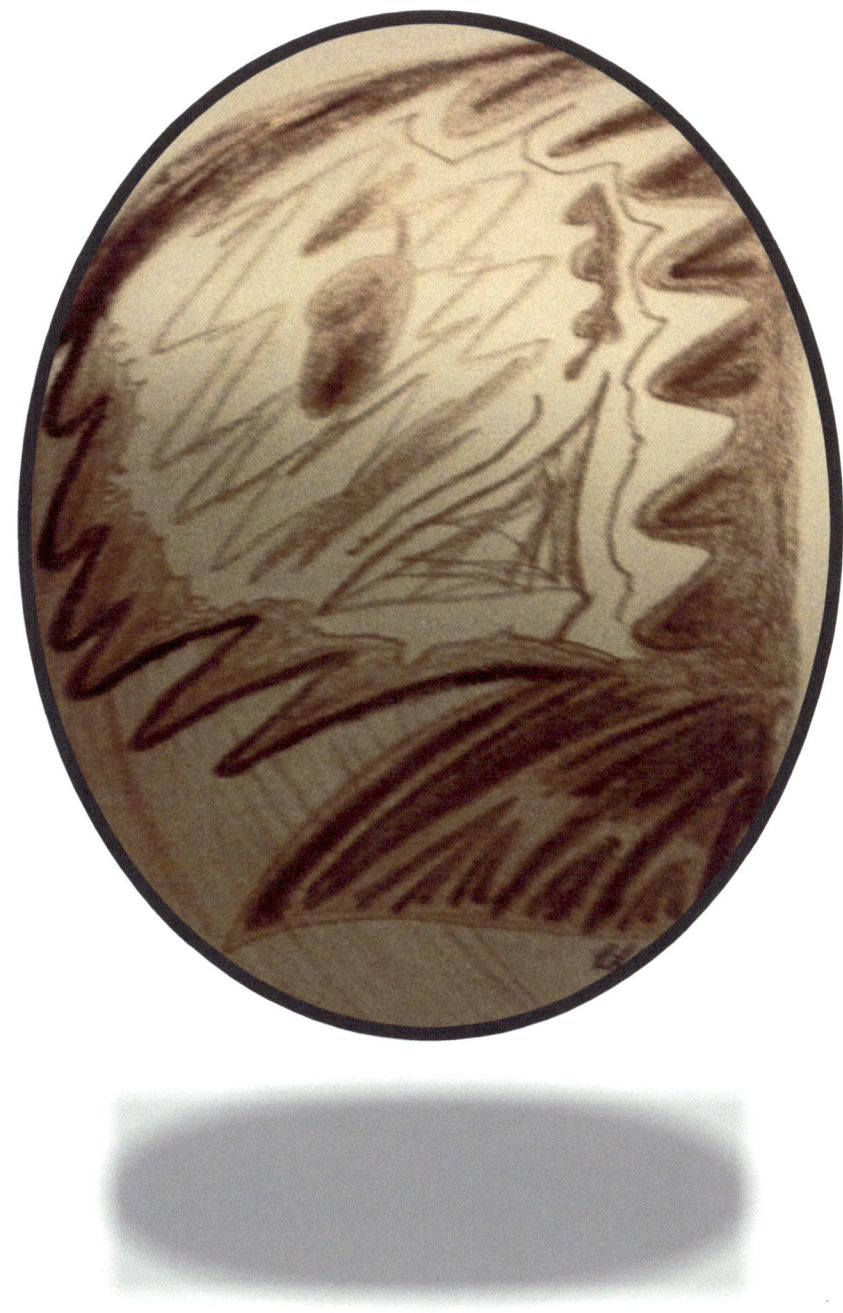

The light bulb keeps going off…it has a bright blue flame…

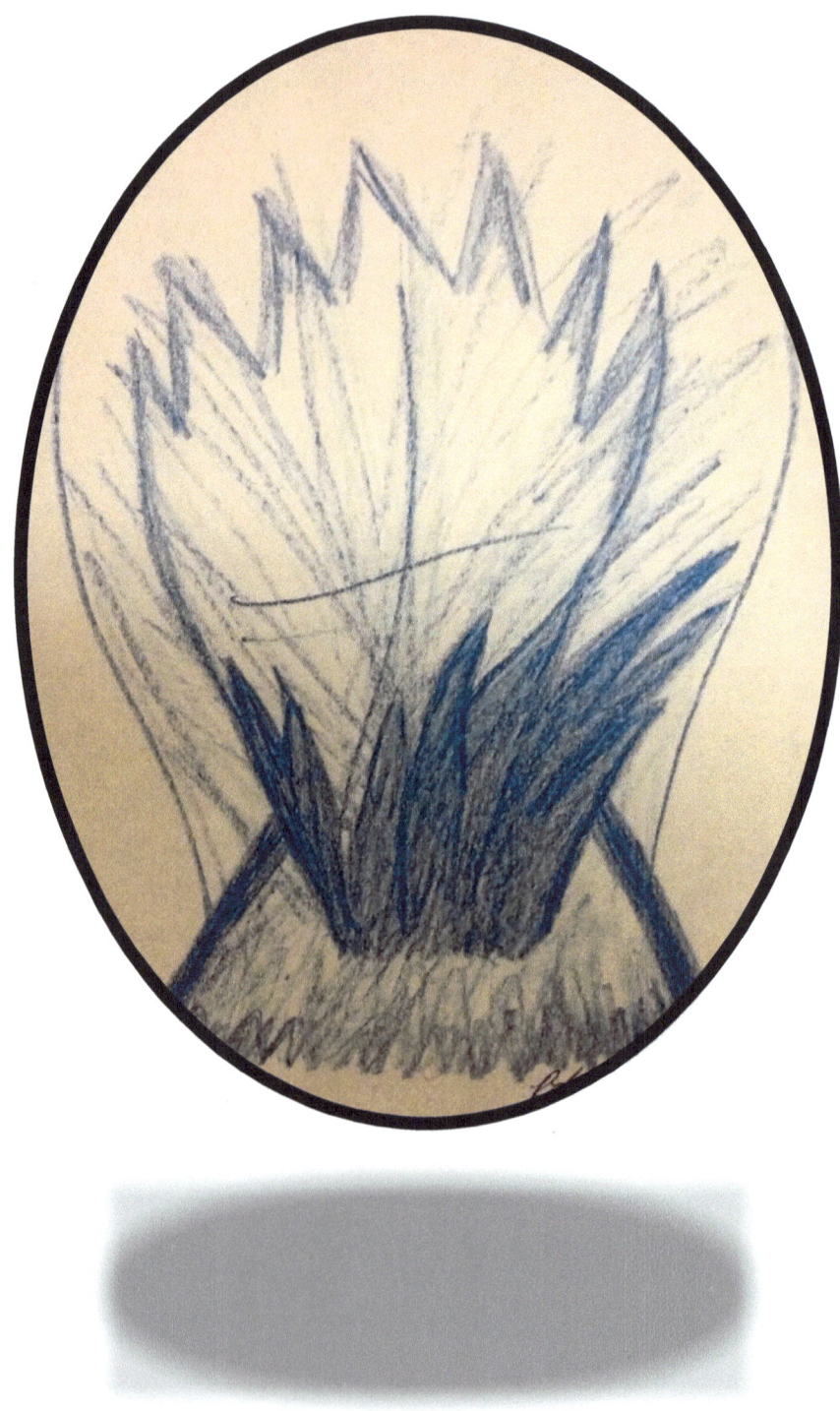

It won't be a secret for long. My house is already caught in the whirlwind…

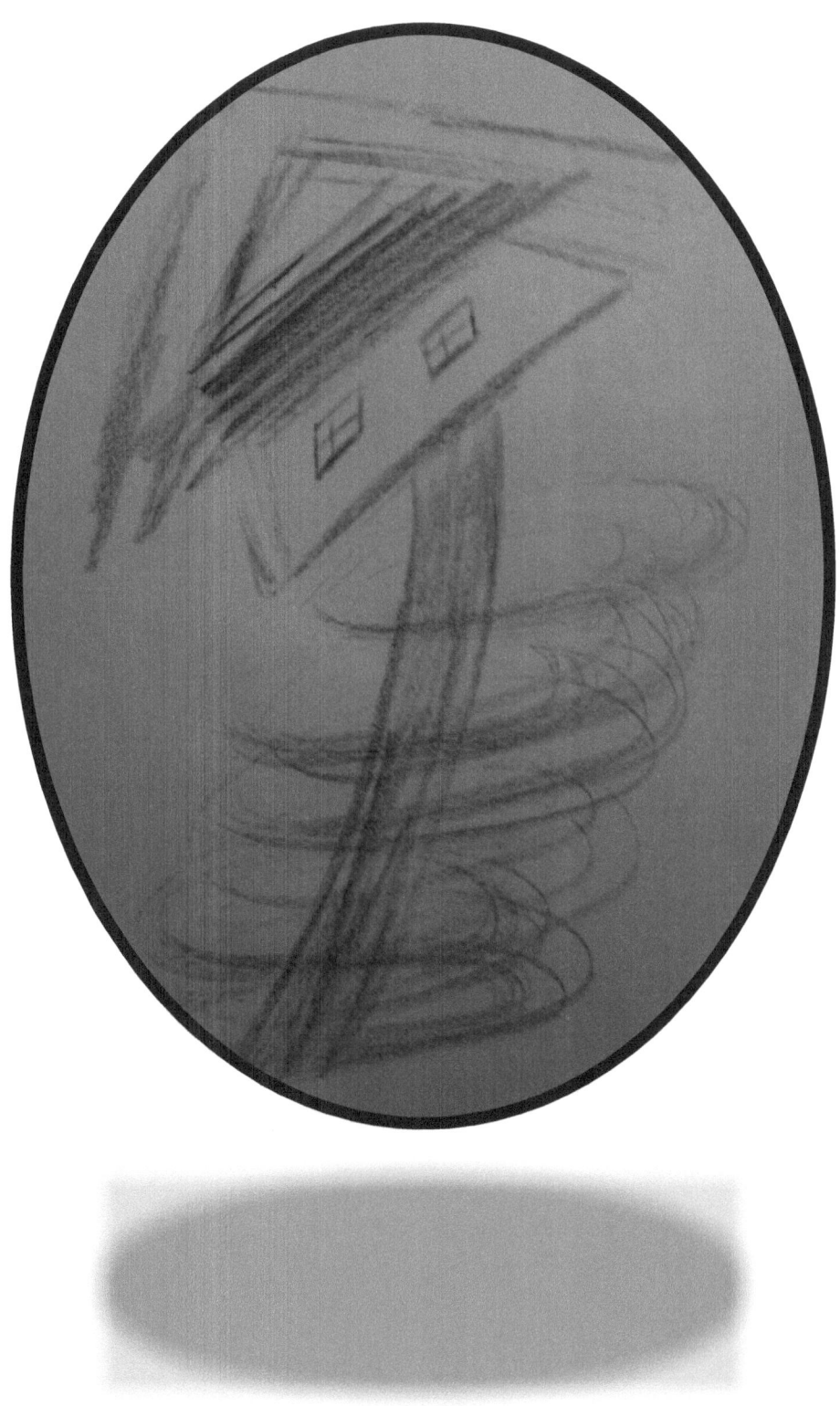

The birds are pointing this way…

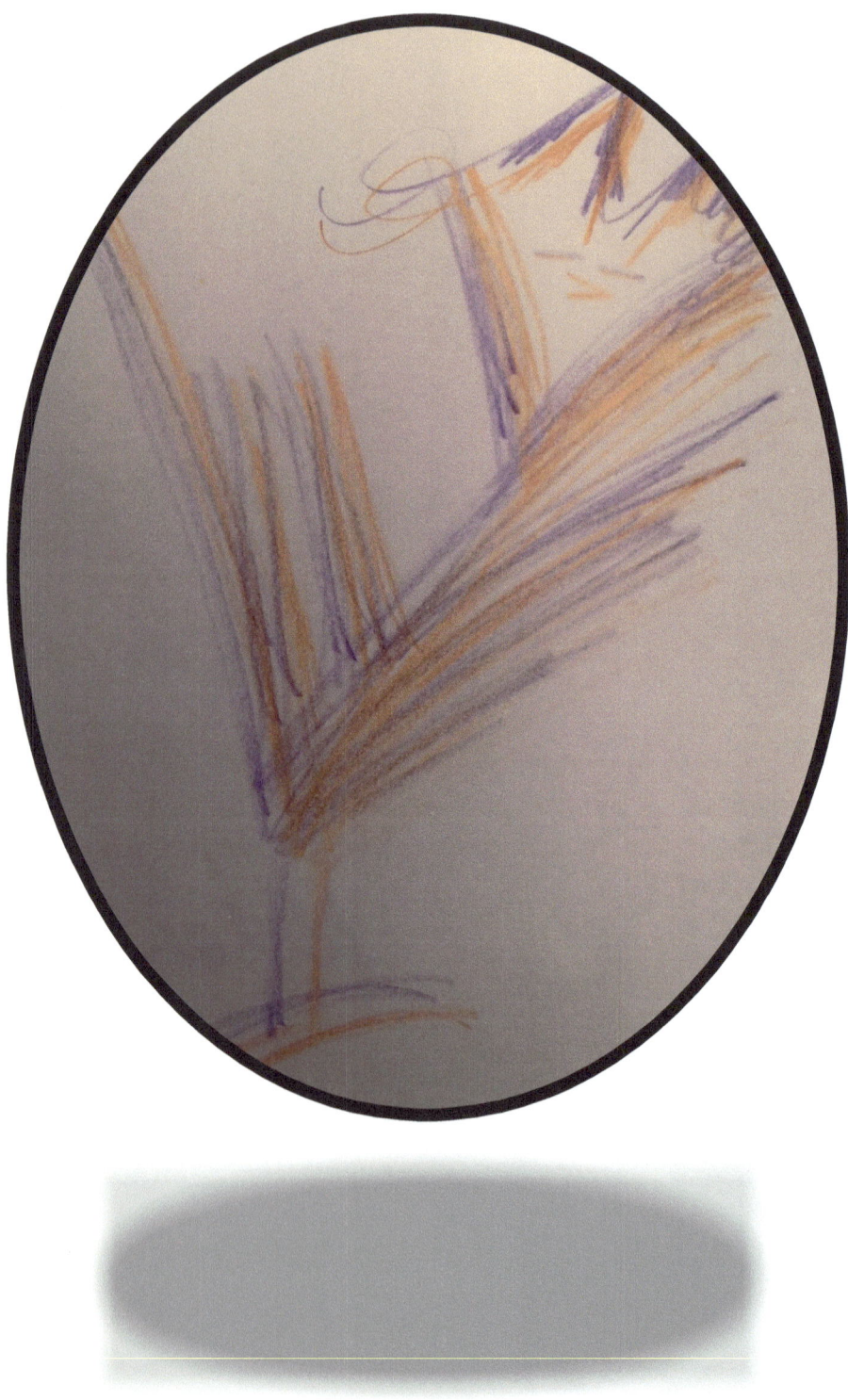

They can see the angel bluebird that carries the window of opportunity…

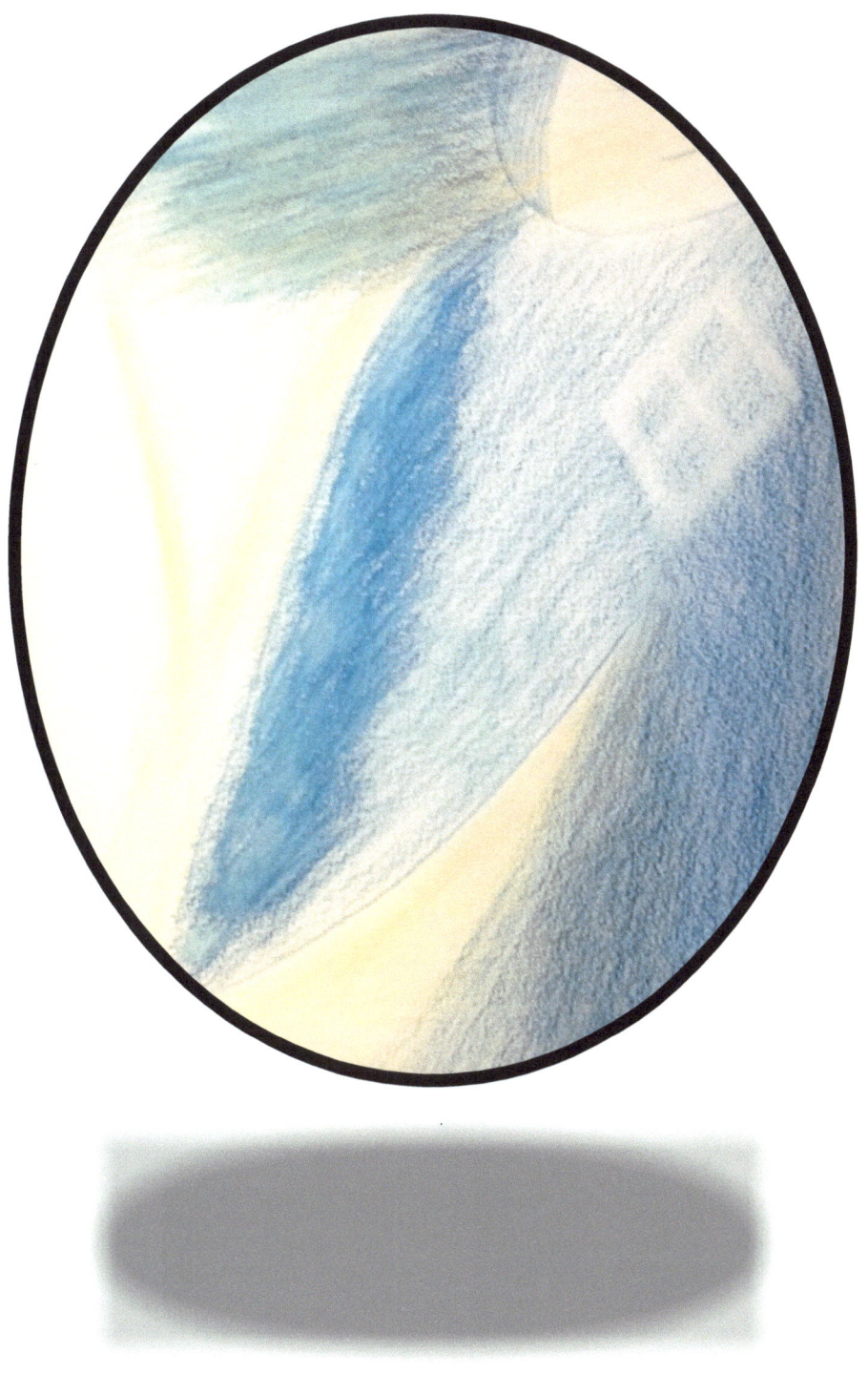

"secret Life OV an antE" by RL Lane…

Ante – before. Did someone before me have a secret life?!

Well, it wasn't a secret to everyone.

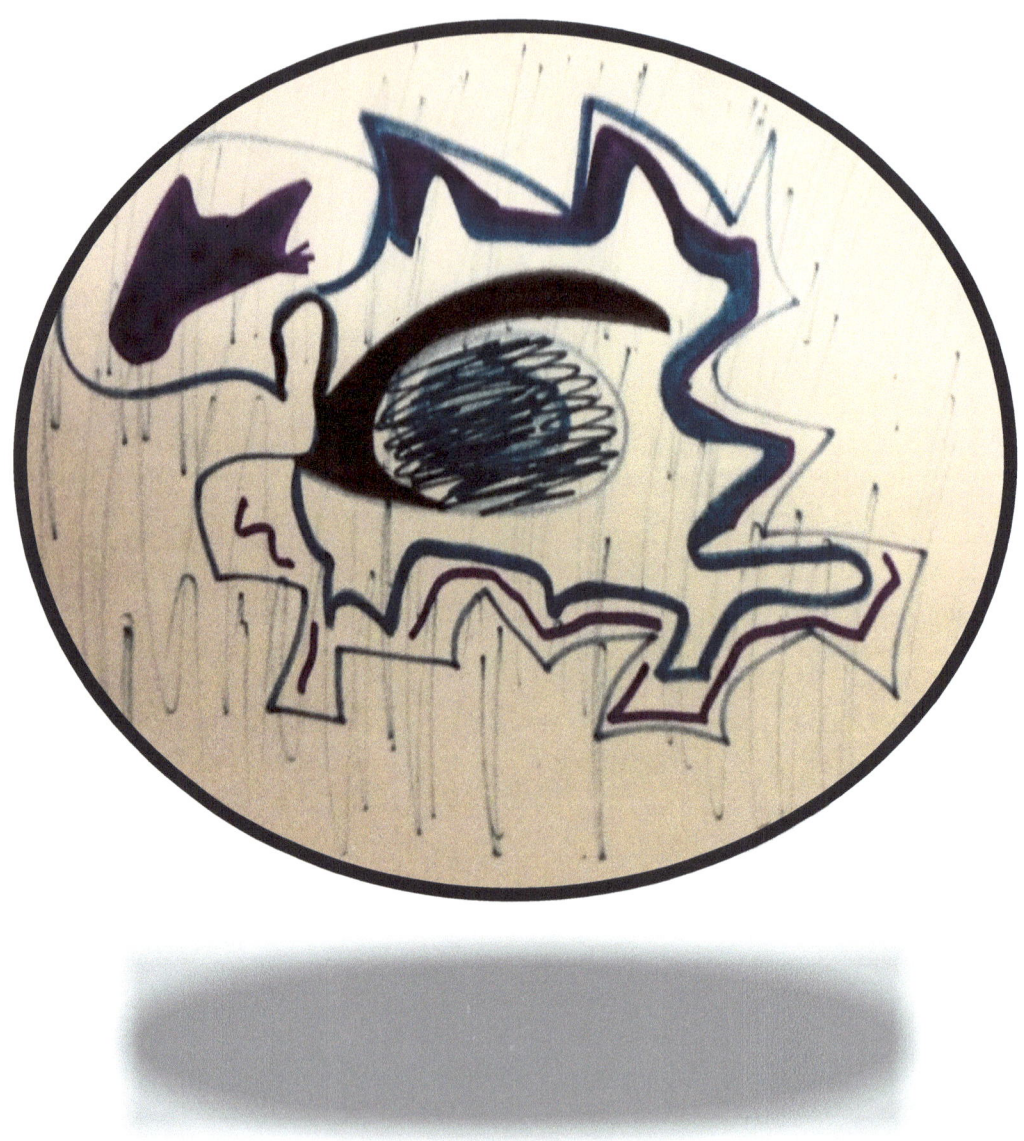

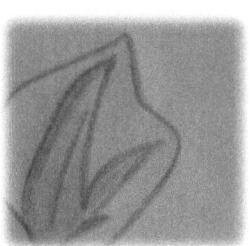

ISBN: 1512388610
ISBN-13: 978-1512388619

www.ingramcontent.com/pod-product-compliance
Lightning Source LLC
Chambersburg PA
CBHW050437180526
45159CB00006B/2570